BLUE MIND'S FLOWER

BLUE MIND'S FLOWER

Janet Read

MOONSTONE PRESS

Some of the poems in this collection originally appeared in *The New Quarterly* and in *Other Voices.*

Cover art: Brenda Clark, *Vision Fugitive X,* pastel; by permission of the artist.
Author photograph courtesy *Oshawa Times.*
Designed and set by ECW *Type & Art,* Oakville.
Printed on Zephyr Antique Laid, sewn into signatures, and bound by The Porcupine's Quill, Inc., Erin, Ontario.

Moonstone Press gratefully acknowledges the ongoing support of The Canada Council and the Ontario Arts Council.

CANADIAN CATALOGUING IN PUBLICATION DATA

Read, Janet, 1956–
Blue mind's flower

Poems.
ISBN 0-920259-41-3

I. Title.

PS8585.E33B5 1992 C811'.54 C92-093882-5
PR9199.3.R43B5 1992

Moonstone Press
175 Brock Street
Goderich, Ontario
Canada N7A 1R4

for my family,

and in memory of Elsie

A house for wisdom; a field for revelation.
Speak to the stones, and the stars answer.
At first the visible obscures:
Go where light is.

— *Theodore Roethke*

CONTENTS

I the palace at 4 am

II rooms, gardens, wilderness . . . .

III fugitive light

IV edge of dreams / landforms

I

the palace at 4 am

some of us are here
because we were visited
at dawn
were given a third
ear

— *Dorothy Livesay*

EURYDICE SPEAKS

1

the sting of the serpent was soft
and lingering as a kiss,
I thought the god had bruised my heel
with his shining mouth.

the dark, sudden,
a hurried descent
into the tangled roots of night.

I am a voice without speech,
dancing
struggling to rise through a white sea
that clings tight as grave cloths
around my bones.

2

I am a memory of love
abandoned, a subject
for painters and musicians:
a sacrifice to myth.

Why did you love me so?
you men and gods,
cupping me like water
in the palm of your desire,

I dropped like a stone
into the pool
of the great shadow.

3

he was glad
and smiled, in the dark,
when I surrendered.

his teeth are white,
his hair is black,
his house is rank
with the dark decay
of the heart.

his skin insists
on the scaffold of bones,
the structure of teeth,
taut wires of muscle
in the claws of his hands,
in the cage of his body.

he wears the death's head
lightly, I imagine it a mask,
a thin disguise of every face
that stalks the mind.

4

I remember you, Orpheus,
your harp, your flute,
silver under the torches
before the colonnaded temples.

the buildings arced towards you,
trees bent their arms to your song,
grew ears instead of leaves,
and birds revolved above your head
in a fantastic dance of clouds.

the people danced in the market,
danced carelessly as leaves
in the wind, or flowers,
within the strict geometry
of streets and houses.

few animals remain in this country,
the city is a web of bars, and grids,
prisons for soft flesh, and hearts.

those few listened,
listened, and breathed
the breath of your song,
your voice; surrounded you:

rats and mice, cats and dogs,
snakes and frogs, furry
creatures I cannot name,
came to the net of your voice,
woven for hearts to catch in;
none escape, the mesh
is fine, very fine.

5

this story tells itself,
(don't look my love)
erects a barricade,
stands, against the fear,

there is the purple sea
around your shoulders,
the blue headlands
and orange dawn
above your hair,

Let us resurrect
beside the Minoan temples
along the Aegean Sea,

you can sing for the bulls,
they will dance
in grace, in beauty,
with slim-waisted boys and girls;
they die lamenting your voice,
and the seduction of your harp.

Let us worship the snake goddesses,
I will dress my hair and cinch my waist:
we will be happy.

(is it too soon
for resurrection?
the name of Lazarus burns the air,
foreshadows the salt of doom
I taste on my lips)

we are a different tale,
bent to another plan.

6

I am silent,
(don't look my love)
the wind blows through me,
my body bends like a reed,
my mouth shapes a tunnel,
my feet are ripples in the pond
where the reeds grow.

my hair is a tissue of clouds
and rain, my eyes are pools
(be blind my love)
of standing water, my lips,
two fish, under the heavy sea,
my breasts are hills,
round under the green grass.

you will not see me
if you turn

I am the breath of wind
stirring the small bones
of the long dead,
rustling under the cathedral
of their ribs,
with a thin dry music.

I am a cedar on the path,
a red cedar (don't look,
my love, don't look)
a stone, a twig,
a leaf, a snail
curled in a spiral shell.

7

the sun circles your hair
and it is gold, the hills
clap their green hands,
the rivers laugh
and the willows dance.

we are filled with light
(look at them)
there is sunlight on the shores
of the blue headland (look!)

I am a voice without speech,
my heart floods your veins
with a red tide under your skin,
my black hair waves
in long fine tresses,
a flag of battle, around you.

8

he falters on the path:
(look at the purple sea,
it ebbs and flows in tides
under the suns and moons of all eternity)

he stops:
(look at the hills
and the willows there,
they are a tent prepared for sleep
and the warm embrace of arms:
see where the bed stands
under the hanging gardens
of the green willow tree)

he turns:
the sun is silver
through his hair,
then white

before the dark

INSIDE THE KEEP

this is love's path
the lines & circles of a maze

each straight corridor curves secretly
through attics, storerooms   memories

there are no bearings, no compass points
but furtive spirals   rooms
the inner chambers of a shell.

I put my ear against cool stone
hear distant sea echo
voices along marble veins

large-eyed creatures are here,
bottom-dwellers,
tenants of the abyss.

fathoms deep inside the keep
cheeks smart, eyes bleed sea water

I go on, my soul a thread
unravelling behind me.

MYTHOLOGIES

I would not be your lady,
stitched tapestries swaying
above the bed

hounds & huntsmen
threading thick forest
calling, calling,
horns like rivers
sounding in the hills

bright blooded ground,
spent stag, fox, boar,
wounded by chivalry.

no keys stream silver
from my wrist, my waist,
or flowers bloom captive

embroidery in my rooms
a rosary of days

* * *

I am a woman in a garden
green-speared, yellow-bloomed where
flowering apple trees, yews

dark cypress twist against the sky;
lords & ladies are beaten into clay
dust of old mythologies.

I will wear flowers in my hair
swim rivers silver with trout
spill down to lake & sea

the antlered moon whitens your hand
lights the passionate bed.

DREAMING DEEP

1

Night flowers bloom
airborne armfuls in rose
red tangled sleep

tendrils curl around my arms
through the small fingered bones

hands pluck cherry petalled
plum blossomed ripe hibiscus buds

leaves are rain
floating the bed
in april green.

2

a terrible energy fuels the night,
my room is a conservatory
a green house, a garden
neglected, a ruin.

Vines scramble over furniture
pull bedposts down
weave themselves among quilt flowers

one leaf here
one shoot there
the whole pattern alive, growing.

I feel their pressure against my back

green tranced
buried in bloom and fragrance
castled by vines and thorns.

3

Star white nicotiana burst over my head
constellations shape themselves

tiger lily, poinsettia, delphinium,
daisies, asters, black-eyed susans,
honeysuckle, lavender, salvia's

red tongued speech
lights the sky.

I am Persephone in a May field
Demeter in standing corn
braiding moonflowers in my hair.

4

Trees tap the window
shadows lattice walls

below this horizon
sun burns green into earth,
wind manifests in the small tremble of new grass

spirit, in the light
dance of butterflies around the stalk.

ANATOMY I

i count your ribs
weave my hand front & back
gently hold your heart.

flayed sinew betrays white
bone tangled ossuary
full of memory & desire

great lantern hearts
burn bright

cage blood moon
sun bones

ANATOMY 2

wind enters the room
shuttles bone on bone

skull round sea stone
warms to my imagined hand

sings & slowly rises
out of the valley of this room

memories of feet dance.

guards hang their guns on trees
brilliant as christmas,
the wind plays them like harps.

sinew, vessels, teeth return,
deeps give up their ghosts

dragon's teeth sprout men
rivers spawn women

oceans sport dolphins, whales
coloured fish & birds.

the wind is full of seeds & fragrance

your hand embraces my shoulder
skin speaks to skin

we sleep

GIACOMETTI'S PALACE

the palace at midnight

time is a great bird
beak bowed against the breast

dense stillness holds
distant rain

heartbeat of thunder

the palace at 1 am

this house is a skull
with empty eyes

somewhere the sound of weeping

the palace at 2 am

the crowd gathers
moves across the piazza
pavement, black & white

pawns in dream games,
their mouths open
reveal secret desires

the forms of animals,
hidden shapes of enemies.

singing forests
spring from stone

people become leaves
whispering in pine branches

you turn to the wind, breathing deep.

the palace at 3 am

my lover's shadow
crosses the pillow

in the moonlight
his eyes are nets

grey thoughts catch there
like small fish

I am tangled in his arms
till morning

the palace at 4 am

the mind dreams columns
trapeze shaped windows

curtains are sea whispers, waves.

ledges are tightropes, are
webs over night canyons.

doors open
to an inherited geography

decipher dry explorer's bones
prophet's skulls!

* * *

bull dancers imagine birds'
flight over curved horns

falling, wounded, broken
arms & legs trail like wings
over the bull's shoulder

awake: he paces dark halls,
            circling

walls tremble
tapered pillars stand
in the earthquake's heart.

* * *

flame leaps sun
cloud rising
tree tops spiral into blue

in the courtyard
a single figure

confronts the dawn.

LETHE

one coin for the ferryman
closed tight in the palm

two pennies shining
skin warm silver
eyes in the night

dark water laps the shore,
you embark, vanish, in a

tide of shadows
carrying shadows.

no memory aches
love ebbs   dies

marked by fossils of desire
floodlines of ancient seas

FALCONER

the heart warbles at the throat
under the breast-bone battlements
spine tower
curtain wall of ribs.

down by the secret river
harp strings hang on willow trees

wind plays in exile
& trees sing.

the falconer's voice
whispers through the trees

unlocks your ribs
draws your soul
through the keyhole of your eye

heart flutters on the palm
flowers in the sky   brilliant

bird in flight.

CONFLAGRATION

soul, without skin shroud
winding sheet of muscle
bright white cage of bone

slips out,
a knife edged wind's
breath under the door

wings thrust in sudden flight:
we are light, the wind & clouds

burning

NAUTILUS

my heart is a shell

sea pulse beats
ghost tides

through small passages
room after room   spiralling
imagined   exits

beware: Ariadne
alarms sleeping minotaur

LETTER TO A LOVED ONE

Entire genealogies sleep here,
inventories of Viking gold,
Elizabethan plate Swiss watches unwound
Jamaican rum Indian spice the
chains and bones of slaves, grim

metals of our time, a gross detritus
building up a new continent among
turquoise & silver trinkets for women
long since married, & buried.

Did they weep? their salt feeding the sea?

Writing letters to dead men,
(we all do that)
sons, six months dead, in exile
in the Arctic or New France,
barred by water from their role as revenants

reliable as clockwork in Victorian fiction
meant to carry messages of sudden death.

There ought to be some current method
as conventional and accurate,

your ghost convincing me,
a few weeks after the event, a

response to all these words.

II

rooms, gardens, wilderness. . . .

. . . the shadows have shifted the chimney
The shadows are pushing the chimney around
The furniture is all changed. . . .

Everything is in holes and pieces.
— *Saint Denys Garneau,* Identité

INTERIORS

I

in this house
rooms are seasons

chairs artifacts, tables memorials
monologues, uprights on a flat ground

place, memory, reveal the heart,
shape mind, make walls, windows, doors

entrance, exit
paths from self

stairs, attics, roofs
shelter, unravel frail threads
visible lives.

grey winter light
curls around cups and saucers,
laps table's edge, dances
broken rainbows, light
shatters calm.

soft willow buds
are tender saboteurs.

2

buds burst green
heart's awakening

sprout knives
carve sun brilliance
to thin-bladed light

shape crimson petals
the soft tulip's mouth

sap bleeds into air
unfolding leaves
sweet rain scent

3

curtains bleach bone-white
hot summer blows
through every crack

dries the wind
booms, quick torrents
rattle in the hills

gutters falling rivers
the house weeping

4

wheat lies lion-bright,
sun bones wasting
long in shadowed grass

leaves wander in the park
nudge benches, statues

slide along paths
exiled lovers
clinging, separating

poems written on leaves
press & rustle at doors
whisper at windows

speak to earth & wind
die in blue fire

5

yellow lily, sun
floats on cloud

water garden
surface of summer leaves
mirrors the secret mind,

in this house
rooms are seasons

LAMENT

my mother's hands
lie folded now
glove-smooth, white.

Lament those hands
collapsed to bone

as skin to skin we touch
& bone is intimate with bone.

I pinned a lily
to the curtain of her room,
orange fire lily, her sun
bright death.

beneath my skin she rages
as childhood's winter kingdom
becomes a vacant house.

Lament those hands,
fallen monuments

pieta made of bone.

HER GARDEN

nothing could grow in that garden,
the soil turned once
crab grass, plantain pushing up
underground resistance.

you were stubborn:
hacking out weed
planting thin-eared corn
marrows, pumpkins that skulked
by salvia palisades;
a hurried luxuriance.

earth needs patient hope
persistent attack,
deep turning, nourishment
from the roots up

promises the mustard seed
the sometime bloom.

WHAT IS HERE?

cup   table
yellow chair
jostle in frames
window   door   room

elements stand for wholes.

what is here?
is there time for contemplation?

cracked cup
three-legged table
yellow striped chair,
the lines of my hand,
bones of my fingers,
house & street escape

slide off the edge of sight
slip around the back of the head.

there are no symbols
only frames and choices,

apertures from the lens of self,
a glimpse

before the shutter clicks

THE PHOTOGRAPHER DEVELOPS YOUR PICTURE

you are wafer-thin
transparent as film

images unreeling
in memory's night.

tracings, negatives
develop: frame by frame,
shadows against a wall.

crop
fade
layer
image
over
image

raise you to flesh
under a red sun
print my kiss
in the twilight of your shadow

let there be tenderness
between us
soft as the hollow
above your collar-bone.

the dream broken
you must not fear
the shattered glass.

touch it gently
it will not splinter
near the heart.

dissolve the shards
in tears
do not collect them.

we dreamers have spun
our shining threads:
& each head pillows
a separate bliss.

not all the fire of love
or bright pain of desire
can shape us
to a single world

we sleep in brittle
palaces of glass.

CIRCUS SUITE

1

Here He Is
cracking his
Long Black Snap

whipping the crowd
round the tent
with the tongue
of his lash.

Crack! Crack!

Children hide,
Adults spill forward, absurd as
Lions' paws, small flowers,
theatre bloomed,

Crack! Crack!

The Show Begins.

2

The Ringmaster grows a Giant
Hat, Black Manhattan Towers, UP!

OVER! THRU Big Top legs, dark
pendulums; his watch & chain mesmerize,
tranquillize sudden fear.

The Lion Tamer APPEARS.

3

Out Stalk Leopards, Lions,
The Tamer dressed in a Loin Cloth,
Bronzed, Fair, Scarred as any
HERO!

his whip, tenderly whispers of meat
& blood and bones,
strokes each cat by a hairsbreadth.

dancing in the circle of their bodies
he never turns his back,
never smiles with his eyes,

cats smile:
Great Smiles,
Belly Wide, Tooth Deep.

4

sad caged shadows, they yawn
in sullen rage, their

ancient anger turned to boredom.

the tamer is too quick
to dress in tiger stripes,
blood red and fresh as meat.

5

Crack!

Whips curl thoughts tent-wise
in and out of cages,

snap skin, flick the mind raw,
wound our heart's desire.

lion heart curls around the lash

& sleeps.

FIVE WINDOWS

1

a window is an eye,
unshuttered, a
gap in the house of self,
gazing out, thin-fingered
into the dark.

it is a hard transparency
built of the bones of aging rocks
fired grain by grain
to a membrane of glass.

the world attacks brick,
destroys a plaster skeleton,
invades this refuge, home.

2

the garden
is a paradisal sphere

where flowering crab,
hyacinth, jack-in-the-pulpit,
are dark and secret
in the angle of the wall.

honeysuckle leaves
tangle fence posts,
make bright summer's festival
leap of root & vine

high-wiring along the fence
pink-spangled
playing green silent games
without a net.

lilies are trumpets
raging against the ripe golden
fall of August wheat

sun embraces earth
fire remembered in winter.

3

the curtained room
where wind breathes in and out,
and light diffuses in silence:

meditation's round stone
tumbles in the drum of mind

grinds between the stones of thought
in the grist-mill of the heart.

six-sided, honeycombed,
ripe with amber thoughts,

a yellow room of pale suns
& golden moons; rain's
innocent speech.

here, white lilies
utter tranquillity

fire learns of ashes.

4

the street limits the frame,
creates the boundary here.

I won't drape this window
black or white, buy pale lace,
flirt with disclosure.

My window, clear and bare
eats up the show like a meal.

I watch, a caged lion or a
meek mewing cat.

In the passing crowd,
In your shell-like clothes
Your layers of animal disguise,

Stand Back!

I May Roar
Swipe You With Taloned Claw
This Window Is Not Lion-Proof!

5

walls of glass reflect
unending views, walls
and windows in infinite regression.

a great pine tree
arcs beside the house,
stabs a thin needle
into a yielding sky

one monument to boundaries.

THE VOYAGE OUT

1

hawk carves blue
elliptical flight
            shore slides away
            slips, in the fold of an eyelid
            over the round sea's edge

            promontories, peninsulas
            islands vanish

            the world is huge
            encloses a vast solitude

this is a voyage

without luggage, passports
without territorial illusions

            buoys clang channel's end
            before rock, reef, wreck

2

it is not easy
the heart's slow journey
through the country of your skin

your hip, tender sickle
curves sky
under hawk's spiral

flight nets
woven by thin-bladed wings

hugging the coast
flower scent drifts out
a green heaviness

against the sour breath of cities,
a green heaviness
salt-tinged, fresh

stars remember compass
sextant, chronometer

eye blind machinery
with celestial compassion

3

navigate narrow strait
cliff, shoal, iceberg's
submerged danger

landfalls rise up
high on curved horizon
invite   repose

dolphins track zig
zag ship's plunge into sea

bone-shaped
clouds drive west

yellow butterflies
orange winged flowers
wi n   d   r   i   f   t

gestures translate words

your arm bridges
hawk's plummet
under bone truss, beam

sounds
sky
deep
fathoms.

LETTERS FROM EXILE

> Exiles are we. Were exiles born. The "far away,"
> language of desert, language of ocean, language of sky,
> as of the unfathomable worlds that lie
> between the apple and the eye,
> these are the only words we learn to say.
>
> — *Conrad Aiken,* A Letter from Li Po

I

I abandon my life

leave rooms with fine brocade
persian carpets mirrors

raise a tent at the city's edge

trees peer myopic green
into this narrow space

plague-ridden carts roll
up streets, down

wind breathes carrion
lovers embrace in arrested decay

I have set out many times
to begin this exile

how many deceptive explorations
lead here
in a willed uncertainty

to a tent under broken pine?

2

winged shapes recede in sky
intricate patterns flight
evade the eye's grasp

learn love's design by touch,
soft skin over necessary bone

I would know you
without sight, hearing
clumsy maps for blind explorers

we have been days together
without food, nourishing

each other feeding on lips
hands, eyes mingling

lost in transparency

3

the little mermaid on knife stilts
dances mortality, her sisters
sing under my window, flying

fish pass like clouds
mermen seek her, grieving

their eyes are coral groves
sea forests   caverns

palaces of drowned continents

4

this exile chose me

I build walls
rooms open into gardens

flowers are meadows
wilderness enclosed

exile is courage
grown in detachment

5

return to the sea
foam waves curl
ride

tide turning
anemones flicker in diffused light

ballet for wind on submarine excursions

6

speak only in poems
citizen of this country

begin again hack
land from cedar swamp

plant fir trees
dig ponds, stock fish
tap trees for maple honey

build aviaries for songbirds
keep bees, grow

domestic in tranquillity

7

my rooms are words

thunder of crickets
in dry evening grass

tree-scream from
green ringed heart
bitten deep by the axe

round years are dry
moon yellow dust

listen:
still water sounds
arrowed flight of fish

spiders highwire
on reflective surfaces

frogs thrust strong bowlegs
under a limpid sky
standing rushes spear pale stars

in all this, a gentle return.

III

fugitive light

memory is a kind
of accomplishment
a sort of renewal
even
an initiation

— *William Carlos Williams*

FOUR POEMS FOR EMILY CARR

I

wings beat silent passage,
dark through green
forest totems

glide
curving down the wind's breath,
turn on sea waves,

barred owl's wings
spanning night

over mountain, sea, forest, valley,
tangled root & stem,

spiral rotted stumps
hollowed by the sharp devouring
axe.

May-apple round
pine-nut brown,
your agile fingers
hold a forest's wounded heart, make

brush strokes, painted shadows
on the retina of memory.

2

victorian menagerie,
bright caravan
sailing the coast

an ark for dying legends
leaping like fish
in the heart's last run

raven spawned,
children celebrate
past time, lost place.

we make the mind's terrain,
build each river, lake, hill,
contour maps,
describe the heart's country.

in the desert
storms are sand
blown in the face
of all our recognitions.

each dies alone
in a skin tent,
making notations,
records of wandering.

no one begins where we began,
diaries chart single explorations.

3

listening, in the long
slumber of your silence

you heard sea
tug against land,

sky tilt westward,
mountain scrape soft cloud

rain forest breathe
under raven cloak,
dark cedar, balsam, pine

green space between the trees,
rustle, whisper the last
retreat of forgotten people,

their names written
in river stones, in clouds,
in the hearts of trees
in fine white bones,
pink salmon scales.

salmon leap
arc against the current
arrow upstream
plunge their death

deep into raven god's bright tears.

4

hold your hand
on the pulse of stones,

feel cloud breath, slow
growth of hills, valleys,

silent houses rotted to dust
fern-bedded oblivion

dream fish leap in our rivers
feathered capes dance
drums beat, masks sing

totems speak.

JONAH

1

three days in the belly of the ocean
lying in a bone-vaulted black rolling crypt

webbed arches of gut
gleam moist with sinew, muscle, bone
rings with the song of his spume
rising up the blow-pipe

into the sky mask of god.

2

in this prison
salt makes the skin grow young
& softens the bones:

there will be a birth
at the end of this.

whale blows
up through green tiered sea
& waves of mountains

he sleeps on the dancing sea
under a sky encrusted with clouds
& birds

he dives
down
down
fathoms below deep
below fathoms

3

there is no escape but birth:
you are a word in the whale's mouth,
his belly heaves in a spasm of speech

& you are spoken on the dry sand
at the hem of the sea,

in the city, the people read your face
like a language; but you, deaf & dumb
decode their gestures to hear your name.

there is no escape but birth:

the body of the whale
one of the wombs of God
on a three days' pilgrimage
to Nineveh.

POEM FOR ADRIAN

(died October 1989, at 14)

it is the woman
your mother, I see
moving in your room
                                        unknotting
shoelaces, folding sweatpants

finding wednesday's underwear
under the bed

matching socks, empty
feet
                                              inside out
gritty
smelling of soccer and dead leaves.

all the poster faces
regard the door, the flat plain
of your bed, straight, tidy
as if you had grown up
yesterday.

she touches objects at random
dresser, bedpost, chair
            buries
her face in your winter coat
            goes away
into numb spaces, tundra cold.

she remembers a child
remembers ruined cities
                                        filled with ash
bodies in doorways, fallen
running in the street
                  sandals unlaced mis-
matched, barefoot.

she wonders
why she must clean this room
sweep ashes

they rain everywhere
sift through closed eyelids

her mouth is a white circle
singing O to the cindery stars

(in my house
two make small breaths
whisper in the night)

I walk the narrow canyons
                they dream
holding each hand
tight.

You Are My Young Lions!
                                        he said
the palm tree in the square moves like a flag

You Are My Young Lions!
                                        he said, speaking
out of earth rock
broken at Robyn Island,
his face is burnt sienna, copper,
the square full of orange light

!POWER!
his arm speaks
!POWER!
palm tree sings
!POWER!
his voice in the throats of his people shouts
!POWER!

one heart beats for all

!CELEBRATION!

the crowd dancing, listens
to the sound of their feet on the road

no easy march to freedom

they drum hard, long, road
dust of their captivity

beat down the bones of their children
into earth drum

it is taut, full-voiced
deep, remembering their flesh

!PUT YOUR EAR TO THE GROUND!

even here, you can hear it
even here, the song in the throat is Mandela

humming, the throat hums, here
where we have forgotten how
to dance with our whole bodies

our white african feet are learning,
tapping out a small rhythm
on unstretched drums

Hear the lion's welcome
See, behind his shoulder

the lioness is smiling!

GUN, STILL LIFE / NATURE MORT, MIXED MEDIA

December 6, 1989. Montreal.

Why write about the bomb?
it is swift silver rain
black dawns, an ultimate silence
like treefall alone in the forest

no witnesses.

Guns are intimate,
fit the palm
pockets
knapsacks
masquerade as books

at universities.

Machine guns fit
the mind like a glove
stutter bullets
shoot words

write bodies.

(posters repeat Alex Colville's
painting along a fence,
Queen Street West)

A man looks out a window,
a ruler and a gun
behind him on a table

a meal,
a kind of celebration, say

gun gun gun gun gun gun gun
gun gun gun gun gun gun gun

PARISIAN COURTYARD

midi

sun plunges like an elevator
ten stories into the courtyard
noon white obelisk

goldfish journey in a small pond
radiant flames in green cloisters
light climbs to a square blue sky

gold discs scatter across the Seine
as St. Germain pierces the sun

quatre heures de l'après midi

tea is a still life
rooted to white ironwork
tables, chairs are arabesques

sun creeps up the wall
slides away
you understand the oubliette's
grey descent, desolation

in strange buildings
spirals under your eyelids.

following the sun
gulls are tattered papers,
kites dancing.

two blocks away
a Jewish restaurant explodes

frontiers, battle lines;
you draw the mind's Maginot line
reject violence, generate

nostalgia for white villages
under green summer leaves, Ontario

corn stands, rifles in the field.

six heures

evening white birds circle
singing towers, courtyards

where newspapers curl
sleepy snails on tables

high up, blue opens
to pink bellied clouds

sun fades sky, drops
over the world's edge

vapour whispers above the river
goldfish dangle in liquid sleep.

Paris, Rue des Pères Saintes, 1980.

ASSEMBLAGE

this house assembles in my sleep
rises up out of air
the lake in the round gilt mirror

rooms shimmer with water
objects live in a skin of light

no single thing casts a shadow.

the sandstone terrace, crumbling
pitted, we use for chalk

scratch our names, bisque
runes on fieldstone.

the wood-shed is ripe with pine & cedar
powdered bark, sweet, dusty

earth scent breathing lilies.

long corridors speak roses
shadow blooms
emerge from walls like whispers, in

afternoon's twilight, conversations;
my mother in company on the terrace.

I am marooned in a blue room:
count cabbage roses
count the bees, peony drunk
beating against the screen, outdoors

the pendulum swing inverts clouds,
imitates flight.

now, lake lit rooms are unhinged brick
& shattered drifts of paper

where lions stalk.

IV

edge of dreams / landforms

When I stood I thought I glimpsed my own desire. The landscape and the animals were like something found at the edge of a dream. The edges of the real landscape became one with the edges of something I had dreamed.

— *Barry Lopez,* Arctic Dreams

PRIMAVERA

willows loose their hair in torrents
crowns spring luxuriant green

apple trees, empty as skulls
make structures for wind

speaking in tongues
among barren branches

the whole country sings
the language of rivers

stones are warm
fragrant as violets

figures in landscape
we hold each other

tangle in slender confusion

* * *

your heart   clockwork
hums behind glass

your eyes light mine like candles
heart stumbles from winter's cave

feels green blood rising
leaves solitude, sleep
dead season's silence

arms entwine
leaves bud from hair

mouths grow roses
violets paint our eyes

we sleep
in summer lilies   fire

* * *

memory delivers time
present   complete
a round world

each moment holds the tail of another
celebrates green time

lakes spawn fish & angels
we speak with men long dead
bones sing
in the furrows of open fields.

world renews
in fine curled petals

bright marigold

UNTITLED

you are intricate
singing from springs

weights   counterweights
fine wires & tiny screws

a locksmith could break your
ribs & silver plumage

bare your heart's whirring
fly-wheeled machine

but you are lovely
& not to be baited

or broken

LEAF WORK

I will hang my soul on a leaf,
graft it
where branches weave close
thoughts in sky, cloud,
shifting wind & rain.

green buds pierce leaf,
pierce veins translucent green,
make blue space, windows for calm.

sun-blazed summer fruit
hangs heavy, passion's proof:

leaf fades under snow
dissolves in clear water

APPLE ROOM TREE

green dappled walls
pink petal drifts
white   cloud windows

shuttered by wind
& amber sun

room
star burnt indigo night
box of shadows
play of leaf & light

tree flames flickering
in the moon's eye

bark skin
rough on hands & cheeks,
tree root stairs, hair roots

weaving beneath pliant ground
dark cellars for dreams.

water mornings
blue light through green
sun holes in the palm
pink blossomed sky

tree in the wind

RAIN'S DESIRE

whale backed ridges
shoal in sea grey sky

purple-budded trees
stretch long fingers,
catafalques for leaves;
desire stirs the land.

stubble whispers in the wind's teeth
speaks through veins of water
ditch & creek springing from old snow

gnarled tree hearts,
hollow in the breast
wait sap rise

fusion: root & stem
gentle rain of leaves

PAPER WHITES

narcissus are white stars
around the pool,
greek myths forgotten in winter's sleep.

water only mirrors sky, the warm blue air
filled with gulls
wheeling over open fields
sown with early seed.

the pond ripples, stares unblinking
into bright sun, reflects the god

explodes in light

JULY RAIN

a distant hum
tingles in the ear
against the window
fine threads, silk

water falls, becomes green

FALL OF TIGER LILIES

brass trumpets
flame tongued petals
green summer concerto

for lilies & sunflowers

sun king hunts a tiger
queen, loves fire lily

bearded sunflower
grieves for crimson

windblown rain on grass.

OCTOBER

moths beat my windows
drum summer's pulse
all season long

night gathers harvest moon
scythed by sleep

leaves parachute
oak mourns, sumac

berries cling,
die in a feast for cardinals.

earth shifts
stars change course,
trees dream green time

snap in sudden frost.

GROUND-LIGHT

each great orange
tree globe shivers

drops, leaf by leaf
tiny faces of the sun

ground-light of november

FIRST WINTER

outside my window
hills shrug quilted snow
close to hollow bones

winter bares its teeth
ragged trees pierce rock

water sleeps in the well
pump sings with ice
butter tastes of cedar.

we light smiles at dusk
hearts are black with cold,

houses narrow to a room
inhabited by strangers

WINTER LIGHT

& everything white
from the ground up

birds flicker to the cherry tree,
fruit dangles crimson

baubles, jewels
on bare limbs.

in winter light the world recedes
stretches thin,

i need the edges of my soul
drawn close as curtains

ROCK

(on the excavation of a granite
boulder from a vanished riverbed)

ghost river runs
beside the house,
twists through night
storms without rain

gives up stones
levered, pried from earth womb,
black granite, grooved
pitted glacial artifact

speaks the language
continents, mountains
stammered at birth,

earthquake's hidden murmur
volcano's quick arousal
sung deep underground.

wind chisel, sun mallet
work granite,
scour & polish edges
smooth from river's long embrace

rain slides over rock
revives ancient voices

SWIMMER

the lake opens
waves cry gull song
mirror sky, clouds

dive
under green tumult,
the dark sings elegies for sun.

blind creatures
nose along old riverbeds,
forest, hills

water follows a private journey
birth through wind, rain

river's long exploration
curled in the sea's belly.

down, down
arms bottle brown

gardens undulate
with your passing

bubbles trail fins
transparent cities form,
rocks, stumps
pebbles imagine wonders.

you try to remember
gills, breath before birth

air

explodes your chest
drives you

up

STONE

I am the stone that faces the sea

crumbling in the long green pull of her arms,
listening to the lovers, quiet by the sea wall.

pick me up
skim me over bright desire

the sea sends me back
back, & I listen. . . .

I am the stone
quarried for the vein
shining riches in my belly

I turn the world to gold
& men who find me buy roses,
buy women, & keep them in glass
vases like flowers:

sometimes the glass shatters
sometimes the women.

I am the stone, knife against skin
of the boy who dreams on the pillow of war.

I am the stone, alone on the beach

keep me in the hollow of your palm
locked in the vault of your ribs.

UNDER THE MOUNTAIN

all summer long
under the high granite
shoulder of the Cascades
& the river plaited
in rapids & falls,

you slept in my arms,
white as moon's cradle.

down from the north, a trapper
with northern river & mountain
glinting in your eyes,

drawn to drown, the music of the bar
flooding the wild out of your veins
with whisky & gin.

I led you home,
a wolverine on a chain,
you loved the cities in my eyes,
traced my body, a map
to thread the wilderness.

but when I looked
your eyes were ice
pale rivers in the boreal forest,
blue-white in a green dark

& all the creatures of the wild in your glance.

STARRY NIGHT

indigo sky braids dark cypress

stars circle east
explode dawn sunflower
cirque de soleil

Vincent waits,
in the whirlwind's eye

BEACH POEM

he searches tide & wreck
combs beach glass
tumbled smooth
in hands of sea & wind

shells
bones
feathers
once, small & intricate,
the white skull of a mouse

he weaves nets
in the dawn by the sea

fish dream of his nets,
made from speech & songs

canopies for absent emperors
fisher kings

LANDSCAPE WITH BLUE FLOWER

there are islands in this solitude,
forests dream in me, lakes
tender at their roots
curl to rivers, arc to sea.

nights bloom stars
fill frost fire white.

green days birth sun-warmed air
pull bulbs from earth
pierce matted grass.

ice melt pours down rutted fields,
fractures light, westward.

there are caves in me,
tunnels
shafts
bolt-holes
places I have scraped through moss

dug down, cradled bedrock,
the body's cadence resolving into sleep,

blue mind's flower, ripening